GW00854411

Cooking with the Chiappa's - H Recipes

By

The Chiappa Family

Table of Contents

This book is dedicated to hard-working cooks everywhere.

Introduction

Hello, we are so glad you chose to purchase this book. The holidays are such a special time a year, when family and friends get together to celebrate love, life and the gift of togetherness. Are you looking for delicious recipes to add to your menu? Do you want to cook a dinner that everybody will enjoy and remember? These holiday recipes can help!

The preparation of a holiday dinner can become a daunting task. There's no need to worry. This book offers a great selection of tasty and healthy ideas that you'll want to try.

In this book you will discover:

- Scrumptious turkey recipes

- Delicious holiday recipes for breakfast, lunch, and dinner

- Holiday snack and dessert recipes

These mouthwatering recipes will give you an arsenal of ideas to present at your holiday celebrations.

So pull up a chair because you are always welcomed at The Chiappa Family's dinner table!

Ginger Ale with Christmas Spices

Ingredients

Cup ginger ale

2 tablespoons rum, with

 Christmas spices (Rum With Christmas Spices)

1 cinnamon stick

1 piece orange peel

Directions

Fill a highball glass with ice.

Add remaining ingredients.

Ginger Ale with Christmas Spices

Baked Stuffed Pasta Shells

Ingredients

12 ounces jumbo pasta shells

1 ¼ cups mozzarella cheese, shredded (Reserve 1/4 cup)

1 cup parmesan cheese, grated

2 lbs. ricotta cheese

4 large eggs, lightly beaten

1 teaspoon black pepper

1 teaspoon garlic powder

1 tablespoon dried parsley

8 ounces spaghetti sauce (jarred or homemade)

Fresh basil, chopped, for garnish

Directions

In an 8 quart pot, bring water to a boil and cook shells for 8 minutes or until al dente.

Drain and cool immediately with cold water.

Drain and place open side down on paper towels.

In a medium bowl, combine the rest of ingredients except the spaghetti sauce.

Reserve the 1/4 cup of Mozzarella.

Place a thin layer of spaghetti sauce into the bottom of a 12 x 9 x 2 inch baking dish.

Preheat oven to 375 degrees Fahrenheit.

Spoon the cheese mixture into each pasta shell and place open side up, in a single layer, in prepared pan.

Pour the rest of sauce over the stuffed shells.

Loosely cover with foil and bake for 40 minutes.

During last 5 minutes of baking, remove foil and sprinkle remaining Mozzarella cheese on top.

Bake 5 more minutes.

Garnish with fresh chopped basil.

Baked Stuffed Pasta Shells

Orange Yummy Brownies

Ingredients

Brownie

1 ½ cups all-purpose flour

2 cups sugar

1 teaspoon salt

1 cup butter, softened

4 eggs

2 teaspoons pure orange extract

1 teaspoon grated orange zest

Glaze

1 cup confectioners' sugar

2 tablespoons orange juice

1 teaspoon grated orange zest

Directions

Preheat oven to 350°F.

Grease a 13 x 9 x 2-inch pan and set aside.

In a mixing bowl, stir together flour, sugar, and salt.

Add butter, eggs, orange extract, and orange zest and beat with a handheld electric mixer until well blended.

Pour batter into prepared pan and bake for 30 minutes, or until light golden brown and set.

Remove from oven and pierce top of entire cake with a fork.

Glaze: Combine all ingredients in a bowl, stirring until smooth.

Pour glaze over cake.

Cool cake and cut into squares.

Orange Yummy Brownies

Bacon Sweet Potatoes

Ingredients

3 slices bacon, diced

½ cup onion, chopped

2 tablespoons butter

1 ½ lbs. sweet potatoes, cut in 1/4-inch slices

1 teaspoon salt

Sugar

Directions

In a large skillet, cook the bacon and onion until tender.

Add remaining ingredients to skillet.

Stir to combine all ingredients.

Cook, stirring occasionally, until sweet potatoes are done.

Bacon Sweet Potatoes

Kahlua Pancakes

Ingredients

1 cup all-purpose flour

1 cup whole wheat flour

2 teaspoons baking powder

1 teaspoon baking soda

1/2 teaspoon salt

2 tablespoons brown sugar

3 eggs

3 tablespoons butter, melted

1 1/2 cups vanilla yogurt, low fat (3 6 oz. containers)

1/3 cup Kahlua

2 tablespoons fresh lemon juice

3/4 cup golden raisin

1 1⁄2 cups apples, peeled, cored and shredded (I used Granny Smith)

1⁄2 cup pecans, toasted

 Maple syrup

Directions

Soak raisins in warm water for 20-30 minutes.

In a medium bowl mix together flours, baking powder, baking soda, salt and brown sugar.

In a large bowel, using an electric mixer, beat eggs until frothy.

Add vanilla yogurt, butter and Kahlua and mix well.

Add flour mixture to the yogurt mixture and beat on medium speed just until blended and smooth.

Place shredded apples in the microwave for 60 seconds.

Drain raisins on paper towels.

Fold raisins and apples into batter and combine well.

If batter is too thick, add a little more yogurt or more Kahlua.

Heat griddle to medium heat (about 350 – 400 F).

Spoon batter, ½ cup at a time, onto hot griddle and spread out to approximately 6-7 Inch pancakes.

Cook for 5-6 minutes or until bubbles form on top.

Flip and cook for another 5-6 minutes or until golden brown.

Serve with toasted pecans and maple syrup. (Some of only used powdered sugar).

Kahlua Pancakes

Zesty Zucchini Wrap

Ingredients

2 zucchini, green and yellow julienned

1 onion, diced

1 red bell pepper, julienned

2 tablespoons olive oil

1 cup Baby Spinach

1/2 cup guacamole

Salt and pepper

Flour tortilla

Cherry tomatoes (optional)

Italian dressing (optional)

Directions

Heat olive oil in a pan.

Add sliced zucchini, bell pepper and onion.

Sauté approximately 10 minutes until done to your taste. Add salt and pepper.

Spread 2 tbsp. guacamole on flour tortilla, or more if you are like me .

Add cooked veggies to the tortilla, spinach and sliced cherry tomatoes if using.

Wrap and serve either hot or cold.

Zesty Zucchini Wrap

Raspberry Chipotle Sauce

Ingredients

2 cups fresh raspberries or 2 cups frozen unsweetened raspberries, thawed

¼ cup sugar

¼ cup ruby port

1 chipotle Chile in adobo, from a 7 ounce can more to taste

Directions

(You can use the adobo the chilies are packed in if you like. It will make it hotter!).

Combine all ingredients in a heavy sauce pan and simmer, stirring occasionally, until sugar is dissolved.

Allow to cool a little if desired.

Transfer to a food processor or blender and blend until sauce is smooth. I use my immersion blender.

Remove seeds from sauce using a fine mesh strainer if desired.

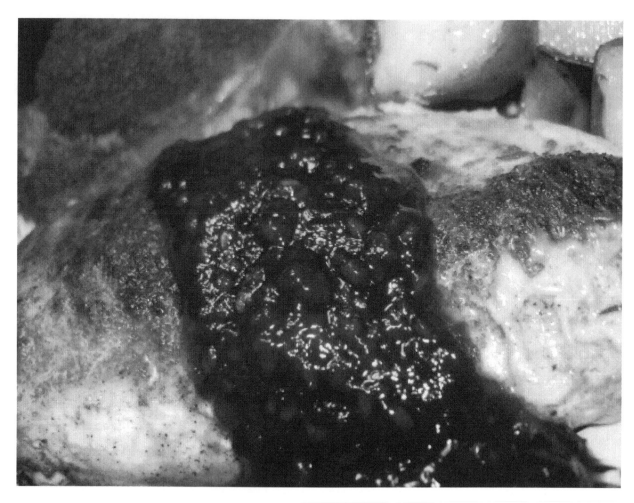

Raspberry Chipotle Sauce

Pineapple Southern Comfort Yummy Martini

Ingredients

1/2cup Southern Comfort

½ cup 100% pineapple juice

Ice

Slice fresh lime

Directions

Place ice in large size/deep martini glass to chill and set aside.

In your favorite shaker pour southern comfort then pineapple juice over ice.

Shake Shake Shake!

Empty ice from martini glass and pour drink (strained) into the chilled glass.

Garnish with lime slice.

Pineapple Southern Comfort Yummy Martini

Roasted Prawns

Ingredients

40 prawns (medium sized)

1/2 cup onion, minced

1/2 cup coriander, minced

1 teaspoon mustard

1/4 teaspoon chili powder

1/2 teaspoon black pepper

2 tablespoons lemon juice

2 tablespoons flour

2 eggs

1 cup breadcrumbs

Directions

Wash the prawns, and drain the water and set aside.

In a bowl combine the rest of the ingredients except for the breadcrumbs.

Mix well to make the marinade.

Place all the prawns in the marinade and set aside for an hour.

Set the oven to roast at 400°F.

Lightly grease a baking pan.

Take a prawn and dip in the breadcrumbs and set on the baking dish. Repeat with the rest of the prawns.

Let it rest for 20 minutes.

Insert the pan into the oven and bake for 20 mins or until crispy.

Roasted Prawns

Honey-Grilled Pork Loin

Ingredients

1 (3 lb.) boneless pork loin roast

2/3 cup soy sauce

1 teaspoon ground ginger

3 garlic cloves, crushed

1/4 cup packed brown sugar

1/3 cup honey

1 1/2 tablespoons sesame oil

Vegetable oil cooking spray

Directions

Trim fat, butterfly roast by cutting lengthwise to 1/2 inch of other side.

Place in dish or large zip-loc.

Combine soy sauce, ginger, and garlic, pour over roast.

Refrigerate 3 hours or more.

Turning occasionally.

Remove roast, discard marinade.

Combine brown sugar, honey and sesame oil in a saucepan.

Cook over low heat until sugar dissolves.

Coat grill rack with cooking spray.

Place roast over medium hot coals (350-400°F).

Brush with mixture.

Cook 20-25 minutes or until meat thermometer reaches 160°F.

Baste frequently.

Honey-Grilled Pork Loin

Patti's Pasta

Ingredients

1 lb. linguine

½ cup olive oil

1 head garlic, peeled and chopped

1 cup shredded parmesan cheese

½ cup toasted pine nuts

1 bunch parsley, chopped

2 -3 tomatoes

 Salt and pepper

Directions

Heat oil and garlic simmer for 7-10 minutes.

Add a pinch of salt and pepper.

Toss oil and garlic with pasta Put chopped parsley on top followed by cheese, tomatoes then pine nuts.

Can be blended or served layered warm or at room temperature.

Patti's Pasta

Balsamic Asparagus with Bacon

Ingredients

1 tablespoon bacon drippings

½ cup onion, diced

3 -5 slices bacon, diced

1 -2 bunch asparagus

1 -2 tablespoon balsamic vinegar

2 teaspoons salt

1 -2 tablespoon brown sugar (optional)

Directions

In a skillet: Sautee onions in the drippings for a couple of minutes then add bacon. Let cook over med. heat for a few minutes.

Add asparagus and vinegar and salt. Let cook for 5- 10 minute over med. heat.

Stir in brown sugar (this is optional but man, it contrasts the vinegar very well) and either: a)cover and cook on stovetop to desired tenderness or b)broil to desired tenderness (He broils his but I live in an apartment w/ limited resources so I just cook in skillet till tender.).

Balsamic Asparagus with Bacon

Sago Pudding

Ingredients

1 7/8 cups sago

2 cups sugar

125 g butter

1 cup milk

2 cups coconut milk

1 cup corn flour (cornstarch)

½ cup custard powder

4 eggs

Directions

Soak sago well in water for a few hours. Pour sago into a pan of boiling water and simmer until transparent.

Wash under running tap. Drain and set aside.

Put 1 liter water and sugar in a saucepan. Slowly bring to boil and add butter, milk and sago, stirring until well blended.

Mix coconut milk with corn flour and custard powder. Gradually stir into boiling sugar mixture. Continue stirring until thickened. Remove from heat.

Add well-beaten eggs and stir until smooth. Pour into heatproof container and place on middle shelf of preheated oven 230°C.

Bake for 25 minutes or until golden brown.

Sago Pudding

Stewed Beef in Smoky Mustard Sauce

Ingredients

1 (1 1/3 kg) beef roast (outside round is what I used)

Marinade

½ teaspoon ground nutmeg

½ teaspoon chili pepper flakes

1 -2 teaspoon thyme

1 -2 teaspoon garlic powder

1 -2 teaspoon onion powder

1 -2 teaspoon oregano

1 -2 teaspoon soy sauce

2 -3 tablespoons paprika

¼-⅓ cup mustard (if you prefer more spice with your beef, you can use Dijon, I used regular)

½-1 cup water (enough liquid to cover meat is needed)

4 -6 tablespoons maple syrup

Directions

Remove all fat, gristle and silver skin from roast.

Slice into 3/4 inch 'steaks'.

Cut each steak into 3/4 inch strips, then cube strips into bite sized pieces.

In a separate bowl, combine marinade ingredients, mix well with whisk.

Add meat to marinade mixture, making sure all meat has been covered by liquid.

Cover bowl with plastic wrap, pressing wrap to touch the marinade meat.

Refrigerate overnight.

Place meat mixture (including all liquid) in slow cooker on low for minimum of 5 hours (best done in the morning for evening dinner). Test one piece after then to see if doneness is to your liking.

Pour off sauce into separate pot and place on stove to boil, adding 3 tbsp thickening agent (equal parts flour or corn starch and cold water). Adjust to desired consistency.

Serve with rice or pasta. Don't forget your veggies!

Stewed Beef in Smoky Mustard Sauce

Sweet and Sour Shrimp En Papillote (In Parchment)

Ingredients

14 ounces pineapple chunks, undrained

2 tablespoons honey

2 tablespoons fresh lemon juice

1 teaspoon low sodium soy sauce

1 teaspoon red wine vinegar

1 teaspoon ketchup

1 teaspoon cornstarch

1 teaspoon gingerroot, peeled and minced

2 cups mushrooms, thinly sliced

1/2 cup green onion, thinly sliced

1 lb. medium shrimp (about 30)

Directions

Preheat oven to 200°C (400°F).

Drain pineapple, reserving juice; set pineapple aside.

In a medium bowl combine the pineapple juice, honey, lemon juice, soy sauce, vinegar, ketchup, cornstarch, and ginger; stir well.

Slice mushrooms and onions.

Cut 6 15-inch squares of parchment paper. Fold each square in half; open each, and divide pineapple chunks and shrimp evenly among squares, placing near the fold.

Top the shrimp with 1/3 cup mushrooms and about 1 tablespoon of green onion.

Drizzle 4 tablespoons pineapple juice mixture over each serving.

Fold paper, and seal edges with narrow folds; place the packets on baking sheets.

Bake for 15 minutes or until the packages are puffed and lightly browned. Serve in the packages.

Sweet and Sour Shrimp En Papillote (In Parchment)

Miniature Napoleons with Eggplant Crème

Ingredients

4 plum tomatoes

1 zucchini

12 cremini mushroom caps (other mushrooms would work fine)

 Tamari or soy sauce

Eggplant Crème

2 small eggplants

2 tablespoons olive oil

2/3 cup raw cashews

1 teaspoon dried Italian herb seasoning (basil, marjoram, oregano, rosemary)

2 garlic cloves

Garnish

12 basil leaves

Olive oil

Balsamic vinegar

Directions

Preheat oven to 300°F.

Slice the tomatoes and zucchini into at least 12 slices (between 1/4 and 1/2 inch think). Place on a parchment-lined cookie sheet. Spay with oil to coat and sprinkle with dried herbs. Bake for 1 hour and 15 minutes.

Add the mushroom caps to the roasted tomato/zucchini sheet. Spray with oil and put about a 1/2 teaspoon of tamari (or soy sauce) in each one. Bake for about 30 more minutes.

While the vegetables are baking, peel and dice the eggplants (I had about 750 grams). Put a couple layers of paper towels in the bottom of a big bowl and microwave the eggplant in two batches for eight minutes each.

Then sauté the eggplants in olive oil for about 10 minutes until cooked and a little brown.

Add eggplants, cashews, and garlic to a food processor and process until very smooth.

To assemble, put a little dot of eggplant crème on the plate to act as an anchor. Place a tomato on top of the anchor and put more eggplant crème on top. Then add zucchini and more crème. Then add mushroom cap and a dot of more crème.

Garnish with basil and a bit tomato. Drizzle a little olive oil and some dots of vinegar on the plate to really be fancy.

(I found that if the mushrooms are big, they make a better base than topper.).

Miniature Napoleons with Eggplant Crème

Tomato Risotto

Ingredients

60 g butter

1 tablespoon olive oil

1 big onion, diced

2 fat garlic cloves, chopped finely

2 cups Arborio rice

1 (400 g) can tomatoes, chopped

1 cup red wine

2 tablespoons mixed herbs

2 -3 bay leaves

6 -7 cups chicken stock (I mixed with chicken and vegetable stock, just enough stock to cook rice)

3 tablespoons Mediterranean tomato chutney

3 tablespoons Kalamata olives with sun-dried tomatoes and garlic in oil (I bought it in a jar)

1 tablespoon basil pesto

½ cup roughly chopped roasted red capsicum

1 cup blue cheese (grated)

Directions

Simmer stock and keep it side.

In a large heavy pan, melt the butter & oil, cook garlic and onion for about 2-3 minutes, or until onion become soft and clear.

Add the rice and sauté it too until it becomes translucent (this will take 7-10 minutes), stirring constantly to keep it from sticking.

Deglaze with the red wine, and once the wine has evaporated completely, add tomato and a ladle of simmering broth and pour 1 cup stock. Add rest of the ingredients except blue cheese.

Stir stock in the next before all the liquid is absorbed.

Continue cooking, stirring and adding broth as the rice absorbs it, until the rice barely reaches the al dente stage.

Tomato Risotto

Sicilian Holiday

Ingredients

1 ounce Amaretto

1 ounce mango rum

4 ounces blood orange juice

Directions

Pour all ingredients into a glass.

Stir and fill with ice.

Sicilian Holiday

Cranberry Cheese Holiday Dip

Ingredients

1 (16 ounce) can whole berry cranberry sauce

1/2 cup sugar

1/3 cup onion, minced

2 tablespoons horseradish

1/2 teaspoon salt

1 (8 ounce) package cream cheese, room temp

Directions

Combine cranberries, sugar, onion, horseradish, and salt in a saucepan.

Stir constantly and bring to a boil.

Chill for at least 1 hour.

Place cream cheese on a platter. Spoon cranberry mixture over the top.

Serve with crackers. May be made up to 3 days ahead.

Cranberry Cheese Holiday Dip

Funky Chicken with Sesame Noodles

Ingredients

Sesame Noodles

1 lb. spaghetti (get the thinnest spaghetti you can find)

½ cup soy sauce

¼ cup sesame oil (some reviewers have said that 1/2 cup of oil is too much and have halved the amount, so use your own)

⅓ cup sugar

3 scallions, thinly sliced

¼ cup sesame seeds (or more)

Funky Chicken

¼ cup soy sauce

¼ cup teriyaki sauce

2 garlic cloves, minced

¼ cup brown sugar

1 teaspoon fresh ginger, chopped (or 1/4 teaspoon dried)

4 boneless skinless chicken breasts

Sesame oil, for sautéing

Funky Chicken with Sesame Noodles

Honey Ginger Grilled Salmon

Ingredients

1 teaspoon ground ginger

1 teaspoon garlic powder

1/3 cup reduced sodium soy sauce

1/3 cup orange juice

1/4 cup honey

1 green onion, chopped

1 1/2 lbs. salmon fillets

Directions

In a large self-closing plastic bag, combine first six ingredients; mix well.

Place salmon in bag and seal tightly.

Turn bag gently to distribute marinade.

Refrigerate 15 minutes or up to 30 minutes for stronger flavor.

Turn bag occasionally.

Lightly grease grill rack.

Preheat grill to medium heat.

Remove salmon from marinade; reserve the marinade.

Grill 12-15 minutes per inch of thickness or until fish flakes easily with a fork.

Brush with reserved marinade up until the last 5 minutes of cooking time.

Discard leftover marinade.

Honey Ginger Grilled Salmon

Cream Cheese Cinnamon Crescents

Ingredients

2 (8 ounce) cans crescent roll dough

2 (8 ounce) packages cream cheese

1 3⁄4 cups sugar

1 teaspoon vanilla

1⁄2 cup butter

1 teaspoon cinnamon

Directions

Roll out one can of crescent rolls in bottom of 9x13 pan.

I sprayed pan with cooking spray.

Cream together: 2 8oz. cream cheese.

1 cup sugar.

1 teaspoon vanilla.

Spread this mixture over crescent rolls.

Lay second tube of crescent rolls over mixture.

Melt 1/2 cup butter, mix in 3/4 cup sugar,

1 teaspoon cinnamon, and pour over top.

Bake at 350° for 30-35 minutes.

Cream Cheese Cinnamon Crescents

Roasted Pumpkin Seeds

Ingredients

1 ½ cups pumpkin seeds

2 teaspoons melted butter (olive oil or vegetable oil work well) or 2 teaspoons melted oil (olive oil or vegetable oil work well)

Salt

Garlic powder (optional)

Cayenne pepper (optional)

Seasoning salt (optional)

Cajun seasoning (optional)

Directions

Preheat oven to 300 degrees F.

While it's OK to leave some strings and pulp on your seeds (it adds flavor) clean off any major chunks.

Toss pumpkin seeds in a bowl with the melted butter or oil and seasonings of your choice.

Spread pumpkin seeds in a single layer on baking sheet.

Bake for about 45 minutes, stirring occasionally, until golden brown.

Roasted Pumpkin Seeds

Jello Cookies

Ingredients

1 cup margarine or 3⁄4 cup butter

1⁄2 cup sugar

1 (3 ounce) package Jello gelatin, any flavor

2 eggs

1 teaspoon vanilla

2 1⁄2 cups flour

1 teaspoon baking powder

1 teaspoon salt

Directions

Cream margarine, sugar, jello and eggs together in a medium to large bowl.

Add the rest of the ingredients.

Mix well.

Roll dough into little balls and place on a greased and floured cookie sheet.

Flatten each with a fork.

(Sometimes a little flour on the fork keeps it from sticking).

Bake 6-8 minutes at 350 degrees

Jello Cookies

Onion Parmesan Roasted Red Potatoes

Ingredients

2 lbs. red potatoes, sliced 1/2 inch thick

⅓ cup vegetable oil

1 (1 ounce) envelope dry onion soup mix

Grated parmesan cheese

Pepper

Directions

Combine all ingredients in a large plastic bag, seal and shake until well coated.

Empty bag into a 13x9 dish, cover and bake at 350 degrees for 35 minutes, stirring occasionally.

Uncover and bake 15 minutes longer or until potatoes are tender.

*I think they even taste better more browned and crispy, so you may want to turn up the temp after uncovering and cook them longer.

You could also make this on the grill, covered in foil in an aluminum pan. Grill for 1 hour, turning potatoes occasionally.

Onion Parmesan Roasted Red Potatoes

German Cabbage Casserole

Ingredients

1 lb. lean ground turkey or 1 lb. ground beef, have all worked well or 1 lb. ground pork or 1 cup bulgur (2.5 cups cooked, also known as cracked wheat) or 1 lb. ground chicken, have all worked well

1 medium onion

1 garlic clove, minced, more if desired

2 cups cheddar cheese, shredded

1/2 cup sour cream

1 medium cabbage, chopped

1/2 cup unseasoned breadcrumbs

Salt and pepper

Directions

Brown meat, onion and garlic until meat is no longer pink and onion has turned clear.

Drain grease from pan and discard.

Add cabbage and cover.

Cook until cabbage is clear.

Add cheese and sour cream mixing well.

Pour all into greased casserole and top with bread crumbs.

Bake at 375 for 40 minutes.

NOTE: to freeze- make ahead or re-heat left overs: compliments of Chef Marie Alice: I froze half of this when I originally made it. This freezes excellently and if anything tastes even better after! I reheated it by melting a little butter in a skillet and then crumbling the partially thawed casserole into it, cooking and stirring until it was heated through.

German Cabbage Casserole

Perky Olive Penguins

Ingredients

1 (5 3/4 ounce) can jumbo pitted ripe olives, drained

1 (3 ounce) package cream cheese, softened

1/2 teaspoon dried onion flakes

1/4 teaspoon prepared horseradish

1/8 teaspoon salt

1 dash pepper

1 dash garlic powder

1 medium carrot, cut into 1/4 inch slices

12 small pitted ripe olives

12 toothpicks, with cellophane frilled tops

1 (2 ounce) jar sliced pimientos

Directions

Cut a slit from the top to the bottom of 12 jumbo olives; set aside.

In a mixing bowl, combine the next six ingredients; mix well.

Fill a small heavy-duty plastic bag with cream cheese mixture.

Cut a small hole in the corner of the plastic bag; carefully pipe mixture into jumbo olives.

Set aside.

Cut a small triangle out of each carrot slice; press triangles into small olives for a beak.

On each notched carrot slice, position a jumbo olive so the white chest is lined up with the notch for the feet.

Place the small olive, whole side down, over the jumbo olive so the beak, chest and feet are aligned.

Carefully insert a toothpick through the top of the head into the body and carrot base.

Wrap a pimento around the neck for a scarf.

Perky Olive Penguins

Creamy Pumpkin Pasta

Ingredients

1 small onion, finely chopped

2 garlic cloves, minced

2 tablespoons butter

2 cups pumpkin puree

2 cups chicken broth, made from bouillon

1/4 cup heavy cream

1/2 cup sour cream

1/4 teaspoon nutmeg

1 teaspoon salt

1/4 teaspoon white pepper

2 tablespoons fresh parsley, minced

1/4 cup Romano cheese, shredded

1 lb. penne or 1 lb. rotini pasta

Directions

In a large skillet, sauté the onion and garlic in butter, over medium heat, until soft, not brown.

Whisk in the pumpkin, broth, creams and seasonings to taste.

Simmer 10 minutes, stirring occasionally.

Meanwhile, boil the pasta in salted water until al dente.

Drain pasta and stir into pumpkin, simmering 2-3 minutes more until thick.

Stir in parsley and garnish with Romano, more parsley and pumpkin seeds if desired

Creamy Pumpkin Pasta

Chunky Apple Spice Cake with Vanilla Butter Sauce

Ingredients

½ cup butter, softened

1 cup firmly packed light brown sugar

2 eggs

2 teaspoons pure vanilla extract

1 cup all-purpose flour

1 tablespoon pumpkin pie spice

1 teaspoon ground allspice

½ teaspoon salt

2 cups peeled and chopped apples (Granny Smith or Gala)

½ cup chopped walnuts

½ cup raisins (optional)

1 1⁄2 teaspoons baking powder

Vanilla Butter Sauce

1⁄2 cup butter

1⁄2 cup whipping cream

1 cup firmly packed light brown sugar

2 tablespoons pure vanilla extract

Directions

Preheat oven to 350°F degrees.

Beat butter and brown sugar for 5 minutes in a mixer bowl.

Beat in eggs and vanilla just until blended.

Set aside.

Mix flour, pumpkin pie spice, baking powder, allspice and salt.

Gradually add to sugar mixture; beating until well blended.

Stir in apples, nuts, and raisins, if desired.

Pour into one greased 9-inch baking pan; bake 35-40 minutes or until toothpick inserted in center comes out clean.

Cool on wire rack 10 minutes.

Serve warm with Vanilla Butter Sauce.

Vanilla Butter Sauce:.

Combine butter and whipping cream with brown sugar.

Bring to boil over medium heat.

Reduce heat; simmer 10 minutes or until slightly thickened.

Remove from heat; stir in vanilla.

Serve warm.

Do-ahead Suggestion: The cake and sauce can be prepared and refrigerated separately the day before.

Warm the cake, in the oven, and the sauce, on top of the stove, before serving.

Chunky Apple Spice Cake with
Vanilla Butter Sauce

Holiday Cranberry Butter

Ingredients

1 cup butter, softened

1/3 cup dried cranberries, chopped

1/4 cup honey

2 tablespoons orange zest

1/8 teaspoon salt

Directions

Blend the ingredients one at a time, in order given.

That's it, that simple!

Keeps in the fridge, for up to 2 weeks, or, part of it can be frozen and thawed for later use.

Tip: can whip the softened butter with honey then add the rest of the ingredients.

Holiday Cranberry Butter

Ham Balls

Ingredients

3 cups buttermilk baking mix

1 1/2 cups smoked ham

4 cups sharp cheddar cheese

1/2 cup parmesan cheese

2 teaspoons parsley flakes

2 teaspoons spicy brown mustard

3/4 cup milk (or as needed to be able to form the mixture)

Directions

Heat oven to 350 Fahrenheit.

Lightly grease jelly roll pan, 15 1/2 x 10 1/2 inch.

Mix thoroughly the Bisquick, finely chopped, fully cooked ham, and remaining ingredients.

Shape mixture into 1 inch balls.

Place about 2 inches apart in pan.

Bake 20 to 25 minutes or until brown. Immediately remove from pan. Serve warm.

Ham Balls

Party Chicken Wings

Ingredients

5 lbs. chicken wings

1 (8 ounce) bottle soy sauce

1 lb. brown sugar

1 teaspoon ground ginger

1 teaspoon ground mustard

3 cloves garlic, minced

Directions

mix all ingredients together add chicken wings and marinate for 2 days (I have also marinated for only 1 day) drain marinade and bake at 350 for 1 and 1/2 hours stirring occasionally.

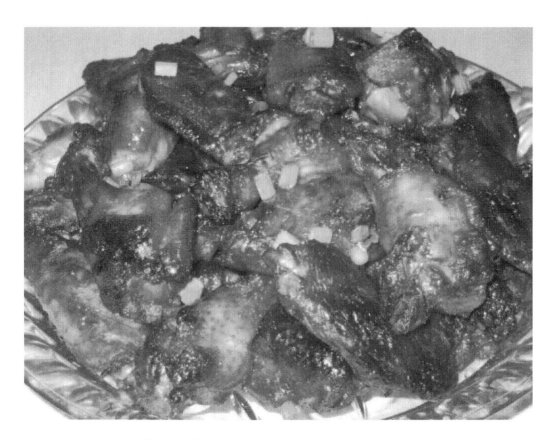

Party Chicken Wings

Chocolate Chocolate Chip Sour Cream Banana Bread

Ingredients

1 cup butter, room temperature

2 cups sugar

2 teaspoons vanilla extract

4 eggs

2 ½ cups flour

½ cup baking cocoa

2 teaspoons baking soda

1 teaspoon salt

4 ripe bananas, mashed

1 cup sour cream

1 cup milk chocolate chips

Directions

Cream the butter, sugar and vanilla together.

Then add the eggs and mix.

Then put in the dry ingredients and mix well.

Add the bananas and sour cream and mix.

Then add in the chocolate chips and pour into 3 greased loaf pans.

Bake at 350 for 1 hour, or until a toothpick that has been inserted into the center comes out clean.

Chocolate Chocolate Chip Sour Cream Banana Bread

Pineapple-Black Bean Enchiladas
Ingredients

2 teaspoons vegetable oil

1 large yellow onion, chopped (about 1 cup)

1 medium red bell pepper, chopped (about 1 cup)

1 (20 ounce) can pineapple tidbits, drained

1/3 cup pineapple juice, reserved

1 (15 ounce) can Progresso black beans, drained, rinsed

1 (4 1/2 ounce) can old el Paso chopped green chilies

1 teaspoon salt

1/2 cup chopped fresh cilantro

3 cups shredded low-fat cheddar cheese (12 oz)

1 (10 ounce) can Old El Paso mild enchilada sauce

8 whole wheat flour tortillas (8 or 9 inch)

½ cup reduced-fat sour cream

8 teaspoons chopped fresh cilantro

Directions

Heat oven to 350°F Spray 13x9-inch (3-quart) glass baking dish with cooking spray. In 12-inch nonstick skillet, heat oil over medium heat. Add onion and bell pepper; cook 4 to 5 minutes or until softened. Stir in pineapple, beans, green chiles and salt. Cook and stir until thoroughly heated. Remove skillet from heat. Stir in 1/2 cup cilantro and 2 cups of the cheese.

Spoon and spread 1 tablespoon enchilada sauce onto each tortilla. Spoon about 3/4 cup vegetable mixture over sauce on each. Roll up tortillas; place seam side down in baking dish.

In small bowl, mix reserved 1/3 cup pineapple juice and remaining enchilada sauce; pour over entire surface of enchiladas in dish. Sprinkle with remaining 1 cup cheese. Spray sheet of foil large enough to cover baking dish with cooking spray; place sprayed side down over baking dish and seal tightly.

Bake 35 to 40 minutes, removing foil during last 5 to 10 minutes of baking, until cheese is melted and sauce is bubbly. Top each baked enchilada with 1 tablespoon sour cream and 1 teaspoon cilantro.

High Altitude (3500-6500 ft): Bake 40-45 minutes, removing foil during last 5 - 10 minutes of baking.

Pineapple-Black Bean Enchiladas

Cucumber and Cream Cheese Appetizers

Ingredients

1 (8 ounce) package cream cheese, softened

1 (5/8 ounce) package good seasons Italian salad dressing mix

1 dash Tabasco sauce

1 (16 ounce) package rye cocktail bread

1 seedless European cucumber, unpeeled

Dried dill (to garnish) or fresh dill (to garnish)

Directions

I wash and score the cucumber with a fork along the entire length of the cucumber, all the way around, to make a design Slice thinly and set aside.

Combine cream cheese, Good Seasonings Italian mix and Tabasco sauce.

Spread cream cheese mixture, generously on each slice of cocktail bread, place slice of cucumber and sprinkle the top with dill.

Cucumber and Cream Cheese Appetizers

Baked Cherry Tomatoes with Parmesan Topping

Ingredients

2 tablespoons extra virgin olive oil

2 pints cherry tomatoes

1 teaspoon salt

1 teaspoon ground black pepper

¼ cup chopped fresh parsley

¼ cup freshly grated parmesan cheese.

Directions

Pour oil into 13x9x2-inch broiler proof ceramic baking dish.

Add tomatoes, turn to coat with oil.

Sprinkle with salt and pepper.

Top with parsley and cheese.

Preheat oven to 400.

Bake tomatoes just until plump and shiny but not split, about 10 minutes.

Preheat broiler.

Broil until tomatoes begin to split and cheese begins to color, about 2 minutes.

Serve hot or warm.

Baked Cherry Tomatoes with Parmesan Topping

Pineapple Meatballs

Ingredients

Meatballs

2 lbs. lean ground beef

2 large eggs

½ cup fine dry breadcrumb

1 teaspoon salt

¼ teaspoon freshly ground black pepper

1 ½ teaspoons Worcestershire sauce

¼ teaspoon garlic powder

Sauce

1 cup packed brown sugar

3 tablespoons cornstarch

1 3⁄4 cups reserved pineapple juice, plus water if necessary to measure (it will be)

1⁄4 cup white vinegar

1 1⁄2 tablespoons soy sauce

1 1⁄2 teaspoons Worcestershire sauce

1 (14 ounce) can pineapple tidbits, juice drained and reserved.

Preheat oven to 350F degrees.

First, make the meatballs: combine all meatball ingredients (there's 7, beef to garlic powder) in a bowl and mix well; shape into 1-inch balls.

Brown them in a nonstick frying pan (I do it in 3 batches) until browned all over; drain on paper towel then place in a large ungreased casserole dish.

To make sauce, combine brown sugar and cornstarch in a large saucepan, then whisk in the 1-3/4 cup pineapple juice/water combination until mixture is smooth.

Add vinegar, soy sauce and Worcestershire sauce; stir.

Simmer, uncovered, on medium-low heat for about 8 minutes, or until thickened.

Pour sauce over meatballs and add pineapple tidbits; stir gently to combine until meatballs are coated with sauce.

Bake in preheated oven for 30 minutes.

Pineapple Meatballs

Stuffed Dill Pickles

Ingredients

1 (48 ounce) jar dill pickles (homemade preferred) or 1 (48 ounce) jar kosher dill pickles

1 (8 ounce) package cream cheese, regular

1 medium onion, very finely chopped

2 large garlic cloves, very finely chopped

3⁄4 teaspoon Tabasco sauce or 3⁄4 teaspoon a hot sauce.

Directions

Cut off both ends of the dill pickles to create a flat surface.

Using a thin potato peeler or a sharp knife Stand the pickles on end on paper toweling and let drain until all liquid is drained, about 30 minutes. In addition, run some rolled paper toweling through the core to remove any liquid that did not drain.

Meanwhile, in a mixing bowl, cream the cheese, add onion and garlic and mix until well blended. Add Tabasco sauce and mix well to blend.

Using a cake decorator or a small spoon, stuff each pickle. Wrap the stuffed pickles in plastic wrap and refrigerate until cheese is firm, about 2 hours.

Before serving, slice pickles into 3/4 inch slices and place slices on a serving plate. (Cover and refrigerate any unused pickles). These pickles are also good for lunches.

You may also add some finely chopped Smoked Salmon to the filling, or some finely chopped black olives, or finely chopped cooked ham. Try mixing equal amounts of Cheese-Whiz and cream cheese, or use the different cream cheese that are available.

Stuffed Dill Pickles

Jalapeno Popper Wonton Puffs

Ingredients

1 (8 ounce) package cream cheese, softened

1 cup Monterey jack cheese, shredded

1 (4 ounce) can jalapeno peppers, diced

1 teaspoon fresh minced garlic

3 green onions, diced

 Black pepper

1 (16 ounce) package wonton wrappers

1 quart vegetable oil (for frying)

Directions

In a medium bowl mix together cream cheese, Monterey jack cheese, jalapeno peppers, garlic and green onions; mix well to combine then season with a little black pepper.

Fill the wonton wrappers with approximately 1 teaspoon cream cheese mixture.

Fold wrappers into triangles then press with a moistened fork to seal (or seal edges as desired).

In a large skillet heat oil over medium-high heat.

Drop 3-4 wontons in at a time into the oil, and quickly fry, turning once until golden brown.

Remove to paper towels.

Jalapeno Popper Wonton Puffs

German Sauerkraut and Potato Balls

Ingredients

4 medium potatoes, peeled and diced

1 small onion, minced

1 (14 1/2 ounce) can sauerkraut, drained and squeezed dry

1 egg

1⁄2 teaspoon salt (to taste)

1⁄4 teaspoon black pepper (to taste)

1⁄4 teaspoon caraway seed

1⁄2 cup all-purpose flour

1⁄3 cup breadcrumbs

Additional egg

Additional flour

Additional breadcrumbs

Directions

Place potatoes in a medium sized saucepan and cover with water; salt lightly.

Bring to a boil over medium heat and cook until fork-tender; drain.

Place potatoes in a large bowl and mash; then allow to cool for 5-10 minutes.

Stir onions, drained sauerkraut, egg, salt, pepper, caraway, flour, and breadcrumbs into potatoes, forming a thick mixture.

Pour some flour in a small bowl; do likewise to some bread crumbs.

Beat 2 eggs in a small bowl also, set aside (Add more egg later if necessary).

Heat deep fryer or oil (several inches deep in a frying skillet) to a temperature of 350 degrees.

Take heaping tablespoonfuls of the potato mixture and roll in flour.

Then coat with egg, then roll in bread crumbs.

Do the same with several others.

Fry balls (which should be the size of large meatballs) in small batches for 2-4 minutes or until golden brown.

Drain on paper toweling, and serve hot.

Makes 25 extra-large balls, or enough to serve about 6 people.

German Sauerkraut and Potato Balls

Warm Christmas Apple Cider Punch

Ingredients

1 gallon apple cider

4 cinnamon sticks

2 navel oranges, sliced down the middle

10 whole cloves

Directions

Pour the cider in a Dutch oven pan, 1/2 at a time.

Put on the stove on simmer.

Add 2 cinnamon sticks.

Add the navel orange slices.

Add 5 whole cloves.

You may not like it like this, you might have to add 1 or 2 more cinnamon sticks or more cloves.

Yummy on the wood stove also.

Take off Heat after approximately 10 minutes.

Warm Christmas Apple Cider Punch

Cranberry Sauce with Port, Rosemary and Dried Figs

Ingredients

1 2/3 cups ruby port

1/4 cup balsamic vinegar

1/4 cup golden brown sugar, packed

8 dried figs, stemmed, chopped

1 sprig fresh rosemary

1/4 teaspoon fresh ground black pepper

1 (12 ounce) bag fresh cranberries

3/4 cup sugar

Directions

Combine first 6 ingredients in medium saucepan and bring to boil, stirring until sugar dissolves.

Reduce heat to low and simmer 10 minutes.

Discard rosemary.

Mix in cranberries and 3/4 cup sugar.

Cook over medium heat until liquid is slightly reduced and berries burst, stirring occasionally, about 6 minutes; cool.

Transfer sauce to bowl; chill.

This recipe yields about 3 1/2 cups.

Cranberry Sauce with Port, Rosemary and Dried Figs

White Chocolate Eggnog Fudge

Ingredients

2 cups sugar

½ cup butter

¾ cup dairy eggnog

3 (3 1/2 ounce) packages white chocolate, confectionery bars broken into pieces

½ teaspoon grated nutmeg

1 (7 ounce) jar marshmallow crème

1 cup chopped pecans

1 teaspoon rum extract

Directions

Yield: 2-1/2 lbs.

Prep Time: 30 minutes

Combine sugar, butter and eggnog in a heavy 2-1/2 to 3 quart saucepan;.

Bring to a full boil, stirring constantly.

Continue boiling 8 to 10 minutes over medium heat or until a candy thermometer reaches 234 degree F, stirring constantly to prevent scorching.

Remove from heat;

Stir in white chocolate pieces and nutmeg until chocolate is

Melted.

Add marshmallow crème, nuts and rum extract.

Beat until well blended.

Pour into buttered 8 or 9 inch square pan.

Cool at room temperature;

Cut into squares.

If fudge is too soft after cooling, chill

White Chocolate Eggnog Fudge

Raisin Walnut Biscotti

Ingredients

Cup butter or ¼ cup margarine, softened

⅔ cup sugar

2 eggs

1 teaspoon vanilla

2 cups all-purpose flour

2 teaspoons baking powder

1 teaspoon ground cinnamon

1 cup chopped walnuts

1 cup raisins

Directions

Preheat oven to 350.

Grease a large cookie sheet.

In a large bowl, beat the butter, sugar, eggs and vanilla together.

Stir in the flour, baking powder and cinnamon.

Add the raisins and walnuts, and stir to blend.

Divide the dough in half.

Shape each half into a long loaf, about 1 1/2 inches thick.

Place the logs onto the prepared cookie sheet.

Flatten slightly.

Bake for 18 to 20 minutes, or until firm.

With a sharp knife, cut the loaves diagonally into 1/2 inch thick slices.

Place the slices cut sided down back onto the cookie sheet.

Bake for about 6 minutes, turn the cookies and bake for another 6 minutes or so until lightly browned.

Cool on a rack.

Raisin Walnut Biscotti

Orange Cottage Cheese Salad

Ingredients

1 (3 ounce) package orange Jell-O, dry

1 (15 ounce) can drained crushed pineapple

1 (8 ounce) carton Cool Whip Topping

1 (12 ounce) container small curd cottage cheese

1 (11 ounce) can drained mandarin oranges

Directions

Sprinkle dry Jello over cottage cheese.

Add fruits and Cool Whip.

Stir together.

Cover and chill until serving time.

We have even substituted raspberries and raspberry Jello with great success.

Orange Cottage Cheese Salad

Black Raspberry Glazed Chicken with Wild Rice Stuffing

Ingredients

8 boneless skinless chicken breast halves, flattened

Salt

Paprika

Garlic powder

1⁄2 cup flour

1⁄2 cup butter

7 ounces long grain and wild rice blend

2 cups chicken broth

1⁄2 cup slivered almonds, toasted

1⁄2 cup seedless black raspberry jam

2 tablespoons frozen orange juice concentrate

1⁄2 cup honey

1 teaspoon finely grated orange rind

Directions

Sprinkle chicken with salt, paprika and garlic powder. Set aside.

Prepare rice according to package directions, substituting broth for water.

Toss rice with almonds. Set aside.

Heat jam, oj concentrate, honey and orange peel in saucepan until blended.

Place some rice on one breast,.

Roll and secure with toothpicks.

Dust with flour.

Repeat with remaining breasts.

Melt butter in 9x13 pan and roll breasts in butter.

Bake 40 minutes at 325°.

Baste with glaze and continue baking and basting until tender, approximately 30 minutes.

Serve with additional rice, if desired.

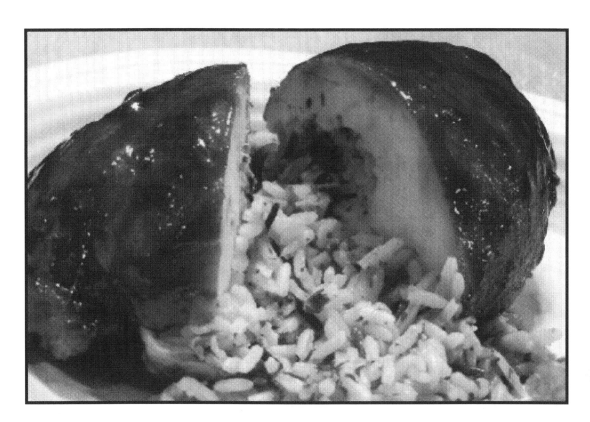

Black Raspberry Glazed Chicken with Wild Rice Stuffing

Perfect Spiced Roast Goose

Ingredients

4 cups water, divided

2/3 cup soy sauce

1 stalk celery, chopped

1/4 cup dried onion flakes or 1 small onion, chopped

1 tablespoon sugar

1 (10 -12 lb.) goose

1 tablespoon salt (or to taste)

1 teaspoon black pepper (or to taste)

2 tablespoons vegetable oil

2 teaspoons cinnamon

1 teaspoon garlic powder

1 teaspoon anise seed

¼ cup cider vinegar

1 tablespoon soy sauce

¼ cup honey

2 teaspoons cornstarch

3 tablespoons cold water

Directions

For the marinade; in a large saucepan combine 2 cups water with 2/3 cups soy sauce, celery, dried onion and 1 tablespoon sugar; bring to a boil, reduce heat and cook uncovered until the celery is tender, stirring frequently.

Cool mixture to room temperature.

Pour the marinade into a large resalable bag; add in whole goose, then seal bag and turn to coat.

Refrigerate for 4 hours turning several times.

After 4 hours of refrigeration time discard marinade.

Sprinkle JUST THE INSIDE of the goose cavity with salt and pepper (you will season the outside of the goose with salt the last 1-1/2 hours of cooking).

Rub the outside of the goose with vegetable oil.

Place goose on a shallow roasting pan.

Set oven to 325 degrees.

In a small cup or bowl combine the cinnamon with garlic powder and aniseed; rub spice mixture all over the outside of the goose.

Bake UNCOVERED for 30 minutes.

Meanwhile while the goose is cooking; in a small saucepan combine the vinegar with 1 tablespoon soy sauce, honey, remaining 2 cups water; bring to a boil, reduce heat and simmer uncovered until reduced by about half.

Remove the goose from oven and baste the goose generously with honey mixture.

Sprinkle lightly with salt.

Return to oven and bake UNCOVERED for another 30 minutes.

Remove from oven and cover with foil and return to oven to bake for about 1-1/2 to 2 more hours or until a meat thermometer reads 180 degrees (basting occasionally with remaining honey mixture if desired).

Let stand covered with foil for about 20 minutes or more before carving (do not prick with a fork or slice during this time or juices will flow out of the goose).

For the gravy; strain pan juices, then skim and discard any fat.

In a small saucepan combine cornstarch with cold water until smooth; whisk into the pan juices and bring to a boil, cook and stir for about 2 minutes or until thickened.

Serve the gravy with the goose.

Perfect Spiced Roast Goose

Shrimp Potato Salad

Ingredients

10 large potatoes

2 cups mayonnaise (Do NOT use fat free or low fat)

1 (6 ounce) can shrimp, drained well and flaked

2 celery ribs, minced fine

1/2 green pepper, minced fine

1 medium carrot, minced fine

20 green olives, minced fine

 Salt and pepper, to taste

 Lettuce leaf

Directions

Rinse off potatoes to clean, and boil in salted water, until fork inserted goes in easily.

Do not over-cook potatoes, or potato salad will be mushy.

When potatoes are done drain right away, peel and let cool.

Put in refrigerator to chill.

When chilled completely, cut them up into med.

sized cubes and put in a lg bowl.

Put back into fridge to keep chilled.

Meanwhile, cut up celery, green pepper, carrots and olives into finely minced pieces.

Add to potato mixture.

Open can of shrimp and drain well.

Rinse off shrimp in the can, and squeeze dry with can cover before removing from can.

Flake shrimp well between fingers and add to potato and veggie mixture.

Mix mayonnaise into salad and add salt and pepper to taste.

Refrigerate until ready to eat.

When ready to serve, place potato salad on a few leaves of lettuce.

Serve with cucumber wedges.

Shrimp Potato Salad

Shopping List:

Printed in Great Britain
by Amazon